United States
Department
of Agriculture

Forest Service

**Rocky Mountain
Research Station**

General Technical Report
RMRS-GTR-205

December 2007

Assessing Post-Fire Values-at-Risk With a New Calculation Tool

David E. Calkin, Kevin D. Hyde, Peter R. Robichaud,
J. Greg Jones, Louise E. Ashmun, Dan Loeffler

I0447033

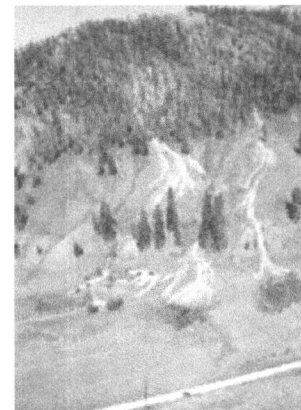

Calkin, David E.; Hyde, Kevin D.; Robichaud, Peter R.; Jones, J. Greg; Ashmun, Louise E.; Loeffler Dan. 2007. **Assessing post-fire values-at-risk with a new calculation tool.** Gen. Tech. Rep. RMRS-GTR-205. Fort Collins, CO: U.S. Department of Agriculture, Forest Service, Rocky Mountain Research Station. 32 p.

Abstract

Wildfire effects include loss of vegetative cover and changes to soil properties that may lead to secondary effects of increased runoff, erosion, flooding, sedimentation, and vulnerability to invasive weeds. These secondary effects may threaten human life and safety, cultural and ecological resources, land use, and existing infrastructure. Current Burned Area Emergency Response (BAER) assessment procedures require identification and valuation of values-at-risk (VAR) from the potential secondary effects of wildfires. However, guidelines to estimate the monetary value of these resources are limited and difficult to apply. This project examined current methods for post-fire assessment of VAR and sought methodologies to standardize and simplify the complex valuation task. A spreadsheet-based "VAR Calculation Tool" supports this valuation framework. It is expected to improve defensibility of VAR valuation and post-fire emergency treatment decisions.

Keywords: Burned Area Emergency Response (BAER), Values-at-Risk, economic assessment, implied value

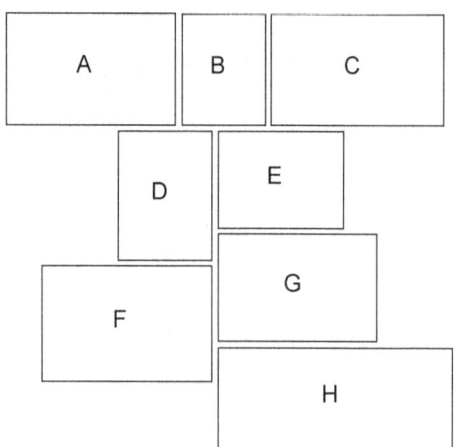

Cover photo credits: A, C, E-G, Kevin Hyde
B-D courtesy of Bitterroot National Forest.

You may order additional copies of this publication by sending your mailing information in label form through one of the following media. Please specify the publication title and series number.

Fort Collins Service Center

Telephone	(970) 498-1392
FAX	(970) 498-1122
E-mail	rschneider@fs.fed.us
Web site	http://www.fs.fed.us/rm/publications
Mailing address	Publications Distribution
	Rocky Mountain Research Station
	240 West Prospect Road
	Fort Collins, CO 80526

Rocky Mountain Research Station
Natural Resources Research Center
2150 Centre Avenue, Building A
Fort Collins, Colorado 80526

The Authors

David E. Calkin is a Research Forester in the Social, Economics, and Decision Science Program located at the Rocky Mountain Research Station's Forestry Sciences Laboratory in Missoula, Montana. He develops processes and tools for assessing economic effects of wildland fire and fuel management activities.

Kevin D. Hyde works as a Landscape and Watershed Analyst and is under contract with the Social, Economics, and Decision Science Program located at the Rocky Mountain Research Station's Forestry Sciences Laboratory in Missoula, Montana. He develops decision support systems for risk-based assessment of wildland fire and post-fire watershed response.

Peter R. Robichaud is a Research Engineer in the Air, Watershed and Aquatics Science Program located at the Rocky Mountain Research Station's Forestry Sciences Laboratory in Moscow, Idaho. He has developed and implemented research protocols for measuring and predicting post-fire runoff and erosion and post-fire mitigation treatment effectiveness.

J. Greg Jones is a Research Forester in the Social, Economics, and Decision Science Program located at the Rocky Mountain Research Station's Forestry Sciences Laboratory in Missoula, Montana. He develops processes and tools for assessing economic efficiency of proposed management activities at both the landscape and project scales.

Louise E. Ashmun is a Civil Engineer in the Air, Watershed and Aquatics Science Program located at the Rocky Mountain Research Station's Forestry Sciences Laboratory in Moscow, Idaho.

Dan Loeffler is an Economist with the College of Forestry and Conservation at the University of Montana-Missoula in Missoula, Montana.

Acknowledgments

We gratefully acknowledge the U.S. Department of Agriculture, Forest Service (USFS) and the U.S. Department of Interior (DOI) Joint Fire Science Program for their support of the JFSP study of how Burned Area Emergency Response (BAER) teams determine the monetary value of resources, or values-at-risk from loss or damage by post-fire events, and the development of the Values at Risk (VAR) Calculation Tool (JSFP grant 05-01-01-09). We also wish to thank the hundreds of DOI and USFS personnel who completed the study survey and the BAER teams who allowed us to observe their work. Their patience with our questions and willingness to test ideas during post-fire assessments made development of the values-at-risk valuation process and support tool possible. We thank William Elliot, Greg Bevenger, Jeff Bruggink, Jeff TenPas, Keith Stockmann, and Sharon Ritter for their helpful reviews. Keith Stockmann and Dave Calkin conducted trial runs of the VAR Calculation Tool on the Poe Cabin and Lewis and Clark complex during the 2007 fire season.

Contents

Introduction 1

    Existing Approaches 2

    Economic Analyses Within the BAER Environment 3

    Justification for VAR Valuation Framework 4

    Recommended Approach 4

Valuation of Post-fire Values-at-Risk—A Conceptual Framework 5

    Threat versus Risk 6

    The Process 6

Preparing to Use the VAR Calculation Tool—Obtaining the Input Parameters 8

    Identifying and Classifying VAR 8

    Mapping VAR-Threat Associations 9

    Probabilities of Threat Occurrence and Treatment Effectiveness 11

    Treatment Costs 14

Using the VAR Calculation Tool 16

    Welcome Page 16

    Gash Creek Fire Example 17

    Gash Creek Fire Information 17

    Preparation for VAR Valuation Within the BAER Process 17

    VAR Area Map Page 18

    Map Zone Worksheets 18

    Summary Page 26

Management Implications 28

    Procedures and Planning for Effective VAR Calculation Tool Use 28

    Support for Post-fire Treatment Decisions and Funding Requests 29

References 29

Appendix A—Calculations Within the VAR Calculation Tool 31

Introduction

Wildfire secondary effects include increased runoff, erosion, flooding, sedimentation, and vulnerability to invasive weeds. These secondary effects often pose threats of loss or damage to life, property, and resources. After wildfires, U.S. Department of Agriculture, Forest Service (USFS) and U.S. Department of Interior (DOI) Burned Area Emergency Response (BAER) teams evaluate the likelihood of threats occurring and recommend immediate actions, such as land treatments, road improvements, and warning systems, that will mitigate threats and reduce their impact.

The current guidelines for BAER team resource valuation procedures are very general (USDA Forest Service 2004, US Department of Interior 2004) and difficult to implement given the limited time and information available for post-fire assessments (Calkin and others 2006). The final calculations are best described as estimates based upon professional judgment (Robichaud and others 2000). The current application of BAER treatment recommendations may not be defensible under the increased scrutiny associated with ongoing cost containment efforts.

Current BAER assessment procedures require identification and quantification of values-at-risk (VAR) from the secondary effects of wildfires, but guidelines to estimate the monetary worth of these values are lacking. The Forest Service Manual, Chapter 2523 (USDA Forest Service 2004) and the DOI Manual, Part 620n Chapter 3 (US Department of Interior 2004) call for BAER assessment teams to submit reports and funding requests that establish justification for treatments through "cost-risk analysis." In the case of the USFS, the BAER team is referred to the "cost-risk analysis worksheet" that requires four basic inputs: 1) probability of the threat occurring without treatment, 2) cost of mitigation treatments, 3) probability that the threat will occur with treatment, and 4) monetary worth of resources at-risk. Recent work, funded by the Joint Fire Science Program, has resulted in the development of the Erosion Risk Management Tool (ERMiT) that can predict two of those four inputs in terms of post-fire erosion—the probabilities of the threat occurring without and with treatment for some common post-fire treatments (Robichaud and others 2006, Robichaud and others 2007). Recently, a comprehensive post-fire treatment guide has been compiled, which includes available treatment installation instructions, effectiveness information, and cost ranges (Napper 2006); however, this information has not been incorporated into the cost-risk analysis worksheet. A methodical and efficient valuation procedure that can provide realistic, reproducible, and defensible cost-value amounts for the identified post-fire VAR is needed.

The increased scrutiny of all wildfire related expenditures requires improvements in benefit-cost accounting systems, including methods to assess values-at-risk. Working under tight timelines, prior to implementing emergency response treatments, BAER teams are required to demonstrate that the worth of values to be protected exceeds the costs of the treatments to be applied. Three fundamental limitations compromise effective calculation of resource values-at-risk: 1) current valuation guidelines are unclear, 2) BAER team members typically have limited training and experience in the field of economics, and 3) data to support direct valuation of specific resources, particularly non-market resource values (for example, sensitive wildlife species, undeveloped recreation, cultural artifacts), are not consistently available.

BAER team applications of available valuation guidelines and procedures vary between fires and produce inconsistent, non-repeatable analyses subject to local bias (Calkin and others 2006). Valuation is hindered by lack of relevant and complete value data. Furthermore, the types of values threatened vary substantially between incidents and the valuation data necessary to complete the calculations may not be accessible within the 7 days allocated to completing initial requests for emergency response funding. Finally, the science to support calculation of non-market values is not sufficiently developed to support calculating monetary worth in the short time frames that constrain BAER team analyses.

In this GTR, we describe a clear and reproducible valuation procedure that can improve the documentation and defensibility of values-at-risk calculations and cost-risk analyses. This VAR valuation framework describes procedures already used by most BAER teams. The proposed methods were developed from direct field observation, surveys with BAER personnel, and recognition of the challenges of the BAER analysis environment.

The Forest Service manual for BAER team operations is currently being rewritten for 2008, which provides an opportunity for the agency to determine what VAR will be covered under the BAER program. This manual and equivalent DOI manuals should provide guidance regarding the values that have been authorized for protection through the BAER program. Any treatment that is recommended within the BAER assessment must have a primary purpose of protecting an authorized BAER value.

Existing Approaches

Currently, USFS and DOI BAER teams use different approaches for cost-risk analysis. USFS BAER teams apply a quantitative approach using benefit-cost analysis, which requires that the expected benefits (or negative outcomes avoided) of the treatment be assigned a monetary value. If the identified benefits (multiplied by the probabilistic reduction in experiencing the negative outcome) calculated in dollars exceeds the costs of a proposed treatment, the activity is justified (in other words, Benefits (B) divided by Cost (C), or the B/C ratio >1). When the resources to be protected can be easily assigned monetary values, such as transportation infrastructure (roads, culverts, and bridges) and timber or grazing leases, benefit-cost analysis is relatively straight-forward and data requirements are not overly burdensome. However, data are often unavailable to quantify the resource benefits of a proposed treatment when the affected resources are non-market values. In these instances, BAER team members may rely on indirect methods to assess values. For instance, if a high intensity rainfall event would result in substantial top soil loss, the team may assign the value of the resource to be protected as the cost of replacing the lost top soil—independent of the values derived by society from the pre-erosion environment. This indirect approach would be appropriate if the restoration treatment described would realistically be undertaken to replace or repair the damaged resource. However, it is unlikely that eroded forest top soil would be replaced, and therefore, this valuation, like many indirect valuations, is not defensible. Without clear, reliable resources or guidelines, BAER teams may assign monetary values to non-market VAR based on professional judgment and past practice. Given the limited literature on monetary value change to non-market resources due to damage from post-fire events and the challenges of transferring existing research to new areas, there is reason for concern regarding the validity of these estimates.

Within the current BAER process, benefit-cost analysis is typically completed near the end of the analysis, making manipulation of benefit-cost analysis to justify proposed treatments a valid concern. Additionally, the USFS procedures aggregate the total benefits and treatment costs for all the BAER recommendations irrespective of any relationship (or lack of relationship) between the various threats, VAR, and mitigation treatments. This can result in treatments that are not economically justified (B/C ratio <1) being subsidized by unrelated, but highly justified (B/C ratio >>1) treatments.

DOI BAER teams apply qualitative analysis ranking the relative importance of the resources to be protected. The qualitative approach is straight-forward and simple to implement. However, it does not inform decision-making on the most important question posed to BAER teams: should a treatment be implemented or not? Qualitative analysis does not demonstrate that a proposed treatment is economically justified and therefore an appropriate investment of public funds.

Economic Analyses Within the BAER Environment

Economic analysis for BAER teams requires evaluating the risk to resources that may be affected by post-fire events. Finney (2005) identifies wildfire risk as the product of the likelihood of an event of a given intensity (threat) times the net value change to the affected resource at the given intensity. However, in current cost-risk worksheets, post-fire responses frequently are identified, but the specific resource value change is not specified (review of past 2500-8 Burned Area Reports by authors). For instance, the likelihood of a significant erosion event is not in itself a risk; the risk is the effect the erosion event will have on valued resources such as municipal water quality, wildlife habitat, and constructed infrastructure. Thus, effective cost-risk assessment necessitates that the probability of a given post-fire event is directly linked to potential damage or loss of valued resources.

Basic economic theory states that when traditional markets are clearly defined, commodity values usually are easily monetized. However, the values of natural ecosystems and ecosystem services are not easily monetized and have been subject to considerable academic debate. Ecosystem functions and the associated outputs of those functions (in other words, goods and services) are often referred to as having non-market characteristics. That is, there is no clear definition of existing markets, no buyers and/or sellers, and therefore no equilibrium prices or dollar values assignable to those ecosystem functions. Further, when traditional markets do not exist, inefficient resource utilization and damage is likely without government intervention (Pigou 1938).

Although there is a substantial body of research on assigning monetary values to forest and rangeland resources, very few of these authors identify the change in value associated with fire or post-fire events (see Venn and Calkin 2007 for a review of the challenges of non-market valuation within the fire environment). In the absence of site specific values for non-market resources, analysts can attempt to use benefit transfer methods (Rosenberger and Loomis 2001). Benefit transfer refers to the adaptation of economic information from a specific site and/or resource to another site with similar resources and conditions. Benefit transfer is a practical way to produce resource valuation estimates when comprehensive research for the site or resource in question is unavailable. However, there are a number of strict requirements that must be met to have confidence in the applicability of benefit transfer methods. These requirements, and the limited number of primary research studies from which to transfer monetary valuations, restrict the application of benefit transfer methods in BAER analyses.

Justification for VAR Valuation Framework

We developed and present in this publication new tools and methods to assess values-at-risk in response to the need for an appropriate valuation of post-fire VAR and economic justification of BAER treatment expenses. The Cost Risk Assessment process used by USFS-BAER is difficult to apply to VAR that cannot be evaluated in strict monetary terms. Ranking the perceived value of identified VAR, the valuation system used by DOI-BAER, does not provide any economic justification for treatment recommendations. In response, we have developed this VAR Calculation Tool. The use of the VAR Calculation Tool not only provides common methods for use by both agencies, but it has the potential to provide less subjective, more consistent (between fires and agencies), and more defensible post-fire emergency assessments for justifying mitigation treatments.

For experienced BAER personnel, the use of the VAR Calculation Tool to implement the VAR valuation framework may initially be more time-intensive than past practice. However, we expect that attention to procedural and planning elements and some practice with the VAR Calculation Tool will quickly make this process efficient. In addition, the VAR Calculation Tool supports a consistent process that is not dependent on knowledge of past practice and will allow new, less experienced team members to function as effectively as their more-experienced peers. The VAR tool will also assist BAER teams in targeting their analyses to those areas where identified VAR exist, which may decrease the time required to complete the overall analysis following fires.

Recommended Approach

Based on our review of the relevant literature and the assessment challenges of the BAER environment, we recommend a hybrid approach for valuation of VAR and proposed treatments during post-fire assessments: a benefit-cost analysis would be used where monetary values are readily available and an Implied Minimum Value (IMV) would be assigned to averting loss of non-market resources. IMV equals the treatment cost divided by the reduction in likelihood of experiencing the negative outcome:

$$IMV = \left(\frac{\text{treatment cost}}{\text{Prob (loss occurring with no treatment)} - \text{Prob (loss occurring with treatment)}} \right)$$

The IMV does not necessarily represent the actual dollar value of the resource loss averted—in fact, the true monetary value need not be defined. The IMV provides a value that the described non-market resource must exceed to suggest that a treatment is an efficient use of taxpayer dollars. Thus, the lower an IMV, the more likely the value of the described resource exceeds this IMV. Use of the IMV to justify a post-fire treatment funding request reflects the BAER team's assessment that avoiding potential damage to the described resource is worth at least the IMV, and therefore, the proposed treatment is a wise investment of public funds. Managers review and approve BAER funding requests and, as a result, they must also determine if the treatment expense is an appropriate use of public funds. We recommend that BAER teams provide sufficiently detailed descriptions of non-market resources deemed worthy of protection so that others, who are not in close proximity, can realistically evaluate the IMV. This hybrid approach integrates the qualitative assessments currently used by DOI with components of the quantitative procedures required by the USFS. The use of IMV removes the USFS requirement of assigning monetary values to non-market resources and does not require USFS BAER teams to acquire any additional data beyond current requirements.

When comparing alternative treatment programs or additive treatments to protect an identified non-market VAR, the program with the lowest IMV is typically the preferred alternative. However, in the case of a unique and highly important non-market VAR, the concept of acceptable risk may need to be evaluated, and treatment programs with higher IMV but lower post-treatment threat may be preferred to programs with a lower IMV but a higher post-treatment threat. For example, an isolated section of critical spawning habitat for an identified T&E species, whose loss could result in species extirpation, may suggest a very low level of acceptable risk. Therefore, a treatment program that reduces the likelihood of loss from the non-treatment level of 55 percent to 5 percent at a treatment cost of $250,000 (resulting in an IMV of $500,000) may be preferred to a treatment that reduces likelihood of loss to only 30 percent at a treatment cost of $25,000 (resulting in an IMV of $100,000). The more expensive treatment (and greater IMV) is preferred because the value of the habitat is deemed to exceed $500,000 and a 30 percent likelihood of loss is considered unacceptable.

The following sections will detail a framework for assessing VAR including: 1) identification and classification of VAR coupled with threats, 2) estimating the probabilities of the occurrence of post-fire threats and treatment success, 3) performance of benefit-cost and IMV analyses to justify treatment recommendations, and 4) application of the VAR Calculation Tool to support use of the VAR valuation framework in an example. The VAR Calculation Tool compares and summarizes values-at-risk, associated threats, and proposed treatments based on resource economics. The final section discusses management implications of using this VAR valuation framework and how the framework may fit with expected trends in BAER reporting, funding, and integration with other aspects of fire management.

Valuation of Post-fire Values-at-Risk—A Conceptual Framework

This VAR valuation framework explicitly describes procedures already used by most BAER teams and will impact the order in which tasks are done more than it will change the tasks themselves. A prescribed procedure and tool for valuation of VAR will focus training and make the BAER process more efficient and transparent. This will be particularly valuable for new personnel, individuals with infrequent BAER responsibilities, and groups working together for the first time.

Threat versus Risk

Use of the proposed framework and support tools will focus post-fire assessments on consequences rather than causes. Characterization of the VAR and how threats could impact VAR will drive the post-fire assessment process. The initial question facing a BAER team will shift from, "What fire-induced changes to the landscape now threaten resources?" to "What resources are threatened by landscape changes and what are the potential losses?"

This shift in emphasis requires that *threat* be clearly differentiated from *risk* and from *values-at-risk* (VAR). By definition, *threat* is the potential to inflict injury or damage, and *risk* is the probability of a loss occurring. *Values-at-risk* are the values or resources at-risk of damage or loss. Responses to a recent survey by 214 BAER personnel revealed some of them commonly confused threats and VAR (table 1). We expect that differentiation of threats and VAR would focus field assessments and could make field time more efficient. For example, an area of high burn severity, as represented by a burned area reflectance classification (BARC) image, would not necessarily need to be validated for soil burn severity if no identified VAR are associated with that burned area. In addition, cautious use of the word *hazard*, often used in the context of both threats and risks, is necessary for clear communication. Hazard, similar to threat, refers to a source of danger or chance that an outcome will occur. Unless a valued resource is in harm's way, a hazard, like a threat, poses no risk.

Table 1. Examples of *threats* and *values-at-risk* that are often confused.

Threat (hazard)	Values-at-Risk
Noxious weeds	Native vegetation Ecosystem diversity Natural forage materials
Soil erosion	Life and safety Water quality Culverts and road system
Landslide	Campground buildings Road structure Road use Aquatic habitat

The Process

At the outset of the BAER assessment process, the BAER team identifies VAR and spatially couples them to probable threats. The team estimates the probabilities of threats occurring in the current post-fire environment as well as the probabilities of threat once a proposed treatment has been implemented. Dollar values for market VAR are obtained from engineers and other sources. The team determines benefit/cost ratios and IMV for all treatment options (table 2). With the exception of calculating the IMV of non-market VAR (Step 8, Table 2), most activities in this framework are typical components of current BAER assessments. However, the order and the intentional nature of each step likely reflect procedural changes as compared to current practice (table 3). These procedural changes provide a coherent and consistent treatment justification process that is explicitly described and supported by the VAR Calculation Tool.

Table 2. The VAR valuation framework steps as implemented with the VAR Calculation Tool.

Step	Process	Leading questions	Examples
1a	Identify VAR with associated threats	What resources are threatened and where are they relative to burned areas?	life and safety, homes, roads, culverts, cultural artifacts, and critical habitat
1b		What are the post-fire threats, given wildfire effects, topography, and climate?	high erosion risk at head of very steep drainage with friable soils
2	Map VAR-threat associations	Where and how are threats posed to critical VAR spatially linked?	burned areas are 2 miles directly upstream from municipal water supply intake
3	VAR valuation	What is the estimated dollar value of each market VAR?	cost to replace, repair, or restore
4	Mitigation plan	What treatments might mitigate threats to VAR?	straw mulch, erosion barriers, culvert upgrades, check dams
5	Treatment costs	What is the cost to implement treatments?	cost per acre to aerial mulch with straw
6	Effectiveness analysis	How much will treatments reduce the likelihood of a threat occurring and/or damage to VAR?	mulching treatment reduces the probability of damage to VAR from 70 to 20 percent (0.7 to 0.2)
7	Benefit-cost	Are market VAR sufficient to justify cost of proposed treatments given the probable success of treatments?	B/C of upsizing an existing culvert and preventing road damage $28,000 at a cost of $16,000 reducing the risk of loss from 90 to 30 percent $$B/C = \frac{loss * \Delta\ Pr(loss)}{cost(\$)} =$$ $28,000 *(.9-.3)/$16,000 = **1.1**
8	Implied Minimum Value	Are non-market VAR sufficient to justify cost of proposed treatments given the probable success of treatments?	IMV of bull trout spawning habitat associated with a $10,000 treatment reduces the likelihood of loss from 70 to 20 percent? $$IMV = \frac{treatment\ costs(\$)}{\Delta\ Pr(loss)} =$$ $10,000/(0.7-0.2)= **$20,000**

Table 3. VAR valuation framework procedural changes and rationale.

Procedural change	Rationale
1. Formally itemize draft list of identified VAR at the first BAER team meeting	- Focus field work on VAR and associated threats - Begin acquiring dollar values for market VAR at outset of a BAER process
2. Spatially link all VAR with associated threats and map the VAR-threat associations	- Linking specific threats to VAR prevents highly cost-effective treatments in one area being used to justify non-cost-effective treatments in another area - Maps add strong support to "where" and "why" treatments are justified - Maps serve as a reference for treatment monitoring
3. Provide qualitative descriptions of the threats to life and safety and VAR-threat associations for non-market VAR	- Reducing substantial threats to life and/or safety are necessary and justified - Assigning dollar values to non-market VAR is not feasible in the short time frame allotted for post-fire assessment - IMV (derived from the cost of treatments and the likelihood of reduced loss) provides a sufficient value statement to justify treatment decisions

Preparing to Use the VAR Calculation Tool— Obtaining the Input Parameters

The majority of the time and effort needed for completion of the VAR valuation and treatment justification is spent on obtaining the following needed input parameters for the VAR Calculation Tool: 1) the identification and classification of VAR (life and safety, non-market, and market), and for market VAR, the estimate of the cost to repair, replace, or restore and/or value of loss of use; 2) threat assessment, including the probability that the threat will occur, and providing a spatial link to VAR; 3) a VAR Area Map, made by grouping related VAR-threat associations into Map Zones; and 4) potential treatment recommendations, including costs of treatments and probabilities of threat occurring after the treatment has been implemented.

The VAR Calculation Tool can be downloaded from the Moscow Forestry Sciences Lab:
http://forest.moscowfsl.wsu.edu/BAERTOOLS

Identifying and Classifying VAR

The first step is to identify and categorize the VAR for loss or damage due to post-fire conditions and responses. Five categories of VAR are considered:

1. Life and safety

2. Non-market: Cultural (for example, archeological artifacts; sacred lands; historic buildings)

3. Non-market: Ecological (for example, water quality; protected species and associated habitat)

4. Market: Direct (for example, bridges; buildings; roads; culverts; timber and grazing permits)

5. Market: Loss of use (for example, access to a fishing lodge and supporting businesses)

The significance of protecting human life and safety is assumed self-evident. Therefore, it is not included in calculations to justify treatments.

Many non-market values are difficult, if not impossible, to replace at any price and, as stated in the introduction, have "no clear definition of existing markets." The distinction between cultural and ecological non-market resources reflects the convention of discriminating between cultural-based human values and values humans place on the natural world. While economic methods exist to estimate the monetary value of some non-market VAR, the time and expertise needed is typically not available to post-fire assessment teams. Further, some suggest that ethical, social, and moral arguments make the assignment of dollar values to these non-market resources inappropriate. Thus, in this VAR valuation framework, no direct assignment of dollar values to non-market VAR is done. Instead, an indirect approach, where the VAR is qualitatively described and assessed in terms of its IMV, is used to justify treatment.

USDA Forest Service RMRS-GTR-205. 2007.

Market VAR are those resources that have established prices through available markets. Total costs to repair, rebuild, or purchase damaged or destroyed resources may be obtained from resource specialists, catalogues and publications, or professional quotes. *Loss of use* is a subset of market VAR where a service or facility cannot be used because of damage to the facility or to access routes to the facility. For example, a washed-out road could prevent access to a remote lodge or favored fishing area. The resort owners and associated service businesses would lose revenue until the road was repaired and reopened. It is often difficult to estimate the dollar value of these *loss-of-use* VAR and, if possible, an expert such as a Forest Service and or BLM regional economist may need to be consulted.

In all cases, the identified VAR should be explicitly linked to the threats that put the value at-risk for damage or loss. These *VAR-threat associations* connect treatment costs to specific VAR protection, which clarifies and facilitates the VAR valuation process.

Mapping VAR-Threat Associations

An important input for the VAR Calculation Tool is the VAR Area Map, created by mapping polygons—one polygon for each identified VAR-threat association. Each polygon is referred to as a *Map Zone* (fig. 1), and the valuation of VAR in each Map Zone is calculated individually on separate worksheet pages within the spreadsheet based VAR Calculation Tool. This ensures that each VAR-threat association is evaluated on its own merits. The number of Map Zones needed for a BAER assessment will vary by the number and locations of VAR, as well as by the size and complexity of the wildfire.

When building Map Zones, the locations of critical habitats, cultural sites, bridges, culverts, and other VAR features are labeled with *Map Link* # identifiers. For example, six threatened road crossings are labeled D1 through D6 in Map Zone D of figure 1. These Map Link numbers will be referenced within the VAR Calculation Tool. It is assumed that drainage and road networks, fire perimeters, and other relevant features will be included on the map. This provides a visual overview of the relationship between identified VAR and the burned area.

Using the burn severity map as a base, a Map Zone can be delineated by drawing a polygon that encloses the area containing a VAR or a cluster of related VAR and the associated threat(s). Geographic units, such as watersheds, areas adjacent to trails or roads, and contiguous habitats, rangelands, or forests, will likely form Map Zones of VAR-threat associations. Map Zones may be adjacent, separated, or overlapping. For example, the threat and the risk occupy the same area when invasive weeds (threat) are already established in an area with a threatened native plant species (VAR). In the case of snag trees lining a road or trail that provides sole access to an isolated community, the Map Zone is an elongated area with the travel route (VAR) surrounded by the snag source area (threat), such as shown in Map Zone A of figure 1. In a spatially separated example, the source area of a flood or debris flow hazard (threat) may be some distance upstream from the location of the public drinking water reservoir (VAR). The Map Zone, in this case, begins at the hydrologic divides of the burned watershed(s) and extends downstream to the reservoir (Map Zone B of fig. 1).

Map Zones may overlap where discrete VAR-threat relationships are clearly described and analyzed as separate units, such as Map Zones A and

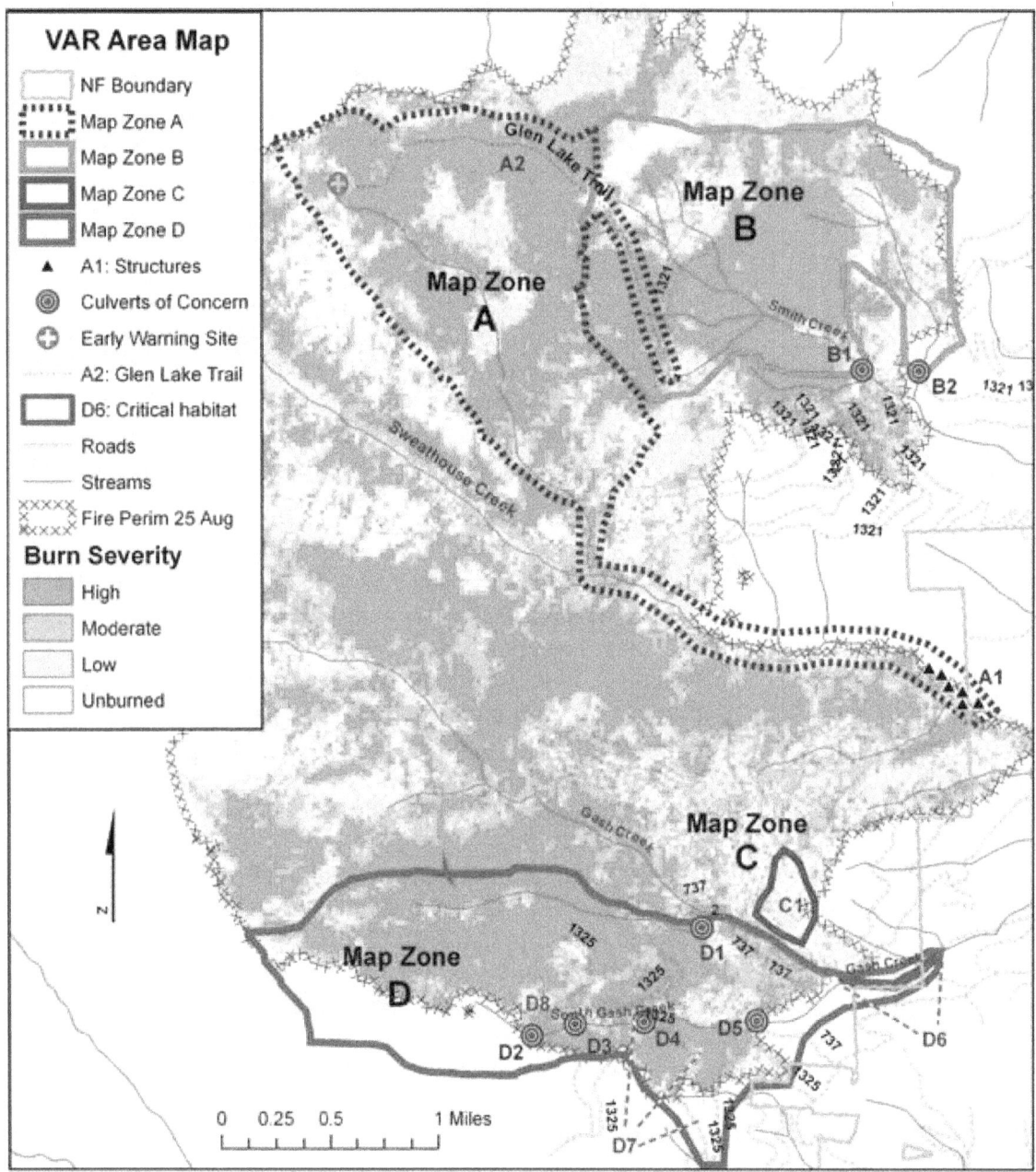

Figure 1. VAR Area Map worksheet from the VAR Calculation Tool showing the Gash Creek Fire example.

B in figure 1. Map Zone A defines a trail lined with burned "hazard trees" that must be cleared for safe access to install an Early Warning System to notify downstream residences that may be damaged by flooding. Zone B defines an area of flooding and erosion threats related to downstream VAR in a different drainage system than the threatened residences. The work necessary to clear the snags near the trail in Zone A will be unrelated to any work that might be proposed to address flooding and erosion threats in Zone B. The two analyses, despite their spatial overlap, will be different and unrelated.

Map Zones are compiled into a master VAR Area Map, providing a visual summary of all the identified VAR-threat associations for the burned area. A map inset may be necessary where VAR are outside the burned area, such as a threatened water supply many miles downstream from the burned area.

USDA Forest Service RMRS-GTR-205. 2007.

Probabilities of Threat Occurrence and Treatment Effectiveness

The VAR Calculation Tool, whether calculating the benefit-cost ratio (for market VAR) or the IMV (for non-market VAR), requires estimating the reduction of the probability of experiencing the post-fire loss due to the proposed treatment. This reduction is defined as the likelihood that the threat will occur under the no-action scenario minus the probability of the threat if the treatment is implemented, until the emergency post-fire threat has abated. Estimating these probabilities is easier for some threats and treatments than for others. For example, the potential erosion after fires can be estimated with erosion prediction models. The Erosion Risk Management Tool (ERMiT) (Robichaud and others 2006, Robichaud and others 2007), specifically designed for use by post-fire assessment teams, can provide the probabilities of erosion occurring and treatment success for several hillslope treatments (seeding, mulching, and erosion barriers). Tools and techniques to predict the probability that invasive weeds will move into a burned area are currently being developed, but are not readily available for use by post-fire assessment teams. For some threats and treatments the probabilities of occurrence and treatment effectiveness will be "best guesses" based on past experience, monitoring results from past fires, research literature, treatment guides and catalogs (for example, BAERCAT—accessed at http://www.fs.fed.us/eng/pubs/pdf/BAERCAT/lo_res/06251801L.pdf, Napper 2006), and expert opinion.

The size and probability of some threats to VAR occurring may be estimated using existing tools and modeling software. For example, the probability of post-fire landslides occurring may be evaluated with a stability model such as LISA (Hammond and others 1992). However, many models do not predict the probability of threat occurrence in the post-fire environment and far fewer can predict the probability of threat once a treatment has been implemented. Nonetheless, the professional judgment of the assessment team may be informed by the model input parameters (generally the most significant parameters related to the identified threat) and the model outputs (predictions). Thus, existing models and tools may provide guidance for assigning reasonable probabilities for use in the VAR Calculation Tool.

Currently, many teams include an estimate of the likelihood that a proposed treatment could be implemented prior to the damaging post-fire event that is being mitigated. If the post-fire event were to occur prior to the expenditure of the money on the treatment, the calculation of B/C ratio and IMV need not be adjusted. However, if the expenditures for the treatment have already occurred (for example, hillslope seeding has been completed but a post-fire rain event occurs prior to sufficient ground cover establishment), the reduction in the likelihood of loss due to treatment should be reduced by the probability that the treatment could be implemented and be effective prior to the post-fire event.

Erosion threat and erosion mitigation treatment effectiveness—Increases in post-wildfire runoff and erosion and resultant flooding and sedimentation are the most frequently encountered threats that must be evaluated by BAER teams (Robichaud and others 2000). USFS BAER teams are currently required to assess post-fire erosion and sedimentation potential regardless of any identified VAR (Part III, Burned Area Report, 2500-8). Treatments that increase the capacity to accommodate runoff and peak flows (for example, up-grading culverts, armoring fill slopes) and treatments to mitigate post-fire erosion (for example, mulching of hillslopes) constitute the majority of BAER treatment expenditures, although invasive weed treatments are becoming more common.

ERMiT was developed to assist BAER teams in the evaluation of post-fire erosion threats and the cost-risk analysis for use of erosion mitigation treatments (Robichaud and others 2006). By incorporating variability in rainfall characteristics, burn severity, and soil characteristics into each prediction, ERMiT provides probabilistic estimates of single-storm, post-fire hillslope erosion. ERMiT uses the Water Erosion Prediction Project (WEPP) technology to estimate event erosion rates on burned and recovering forest, range, and chaparral lands with and without mitigation treatments. The probability of an erosion threat occurring and the probability of treatment success— two parameters needed for use of the VAR Calculation Tool (steps 1b and 6 in table 2)—can be determined from ERMiT output. The ERMiT model is accessed and used on-line (http://forest.moscowfsl.wsu.edu/FSWEPP) and the ERMiT User Manual is available by clicking the documentation icon on the ERMiT input screen or as a written document (Robichaud and others 2007).

Probabilities of post-fire erosion with and without treatments—To use ERMiT effectively, the BAER team must determine the event sediment yield that the VAR can tolerate without sustained damage. For example, if the VAR is a sensitive stream reach with a population of threatened bull trout, the BAER team may determine that any additional sediment will cause sustained damage and thus, set the tolerable limit of event sediment delivery at 0 t ac^{-1}. On the other hand, if the VAR is a less vulnerable stream reach with a reasonable flush rate, the BAER team may determine that a hillslope event sediment yield of 1 t ac^{-1} could be tolerated without sustained damage to the water quality of the stream. The tolerable event sediment yields will likely vary among the identified VAR-erosion threat associations throughout the burned area.

The VAR Calculation Tool requires an input that answers, "What is the likelihood of experiencing the loss with no treatment?" In terms of ERMiT output, this is the probability that the tolerable sediment yield limit will be exceeded in the first year without any treatment. Similarly, the VAR Calculation Tool requires an input for, "What is the likelihood of experiencing loss if treatment occurs." If the treatment being evaluated is seeding, mulching, or erosion barriers (contour-felled logs or straw wattles), ERMiT output includes the probability that the tolerable sediment yield limit will be exceeded in the first year with the treatment in place, which is the probability value needed for the VAR Calculation Tool input.

For example, assume that the BAER team has determined that a portion of hillslope sediment will be deposited in the stream and, depending on the amount, may be detrimental to water quality (VAR). Thus, the BAER team set 1 t ac^{-1} as the tolerable hillslope event sediment yield limit for the ERMiT analysis. VAR Calculation Tool input probabilities can be obtained two ways: 1) by manipulating the interactive "Mitigation Treatment Comparisons" ERMiT output table, the last table in the ERMiT output window (fig. 2); or 2) by accessing the "Sediment yield—probability of exceedance table" (fig. 3). In the interactive "Mitigation Treatment Comparisons" output table (fig. 2), the number in the "probability that sediment yield will be exceeded" box can be changed repeatedly until the first year predicted sediment yield with no treatment just exceeds the tolerable limit, which in this example is 1 t ac^{-1}. Figure 2 shows there is a 50 percent probability that the

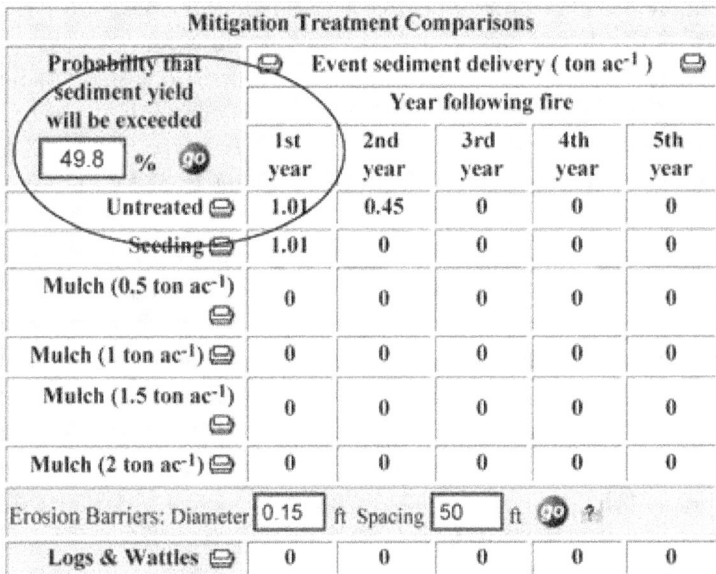

Mitigation Treatment Comparisons					
Probability that sediment yield will be exceeded **49.8** % 🖶	🖶 Event sediment delivery (ton ac⁻¹) 🖶				
	Year following fire				
	1st year	2nd year	3rd year	4th year	5th year
Untreated 🖶	1.01	0.45	0	0	0
Seeding 🖶	1.01	0	0	0	0
Mulch (0.5 ton ac⁻¹) 🖶	0	0	0	0	0
Mulch (1 ton ac⁻¹) 🖶	0	0	0	0	0
Mulch (1.5 ton ac⁻¹) 🖶	0	0	0	0	0
Mulch (2 ton ac⁻¹) 🖶	0	0	0	0	0
Erosion Barriers: Diameter 0.15 ft Spacing 50 ft 🖶 ?					
Logs & Wattles 🖶	0	0	0	0	0

Figure 2. An ERMiT output screen showing the "Probability that sediment yield will be exceeded" that corresponds to just over 1 t ac⁻¹.

Figure 3. Sections of the Sediment yield—probability of exceedance table (accessed through ERMiT output window) showing the exceedance probabilities for 1 t ac⁻¹ event sediment yield.

Erosion Risk Management Tool: Untreated

Bitterroot Valley MT +
sandy loam; 20% rock; 10%, 40%,20% slope; 800 ft; high soil burn severity
[Run ID wepp-16558]

Sediment delivery (ton / ac)	Percent chance that sediment delivery will be exceeded					Permutation Event rank Spatial burn Soil class
	1st year	2nd year	3rd year	4th year	5th year	
27	1.08					5HHH5
22.8	1.15					10HHH5
19.28	1.38	1.02	1.02	1.02		5HHL5
18.96	1.53					5HHH4
18.6	1.73					20HHH5
17.89	1.95	1.04				5LHH5
17.78	2.17	1.06	1.04			5HLH5
17.12	2.4	1.08				10LHH5

90 rows removed

1.2	48.5					20HHH1
1.18		32.57	16.33	9.51	4.06	5LLH2
1.16				4.56		10LLL2
1.12			17.26	10.64	5.88	10LHL1
1.06	49.63	32.66	17.36			75HLH5
1.06		32.76	17.45	10.73	5.97	75LLH5
1.04		34.26	18.95	12.23	7.32	20LLH2
1.01				13.36	8.63	10HLL1
0.99		34.82	19.89	14.48	9.94	10LLH1
0.95			21.39	15.98	11.29	20LHL2
0.92	50.08	35.38	21.95	16.54		5HHL2
0.85				11.34		20LLL4
0.85	53.37	36.76	23.19			50HLH3

event sediment yield will be greater than 1 t ac^{-1}. An alternative way to view this probability is to click on the printer icon next to the word "Untreated" in the first column of the Mitigation Treatment Comparisons table. This accesses the "Sediment yield—probability of exceedance table" (see fig. 3) that lists the "percent chance that sediment delivery will be exceeded" by the sediment yield (t ac^{-1}). Again, the probability that 1 t ac^{-1} will be exceeded is 50 percent (fig. 3).

If the BAER team decides that a 50 percent chance of threat occurrence will require hillslope erosion mitigation treatments, ERMiT output can be used to compare treatment effectiveness among the three types of treatments as well as between the four application rates of straw mulch. Assuming that the BAER team has decided to analyze straw mulch treatment, they can use the output from the same ERMiT run to compare the effectiveness of the four mulching rates. Both methods described above (repeatedly changing the number in the "probability that sediment yield will be exceeded" box [fig. 2] and accessing the "Sediment yield—probability of exceedance" table [fig. 3]) can be used to find the probability of exceedance in the first year with straw mulch; however, accessing the "Sediment yield—probability of exceedance table" is the quickest way to compare treatments. For each mulching rate, the user: 1) clicks on the printer icon in the first column of the Mitigation Treatment Comparisons table to access the "Sediment yield—probability of exceedance table"; 2) finds 1 t ac^{-1} sediment yield; and 3) reads the probability of exceedance in the first year (fig. 4). With 0.5 t ac^{-1} mulch treatment rate, the probability that 1 t ac^{-1} sediment yield will be exceeded is nearly 20 percent, and with 1.0, 1.5, and 2.0 t ac^{-1} mulch treatment rates, the exceedance probabilities are 14, 13, and 12 percent, respectively (fig. 4). Given these probabilities, the BAER team will likely recommend that mulch be applied at 1 t ac^{-1} as doubling the treatment rate (2 t ac^{-1}) and associated costs to obtain a negligible (2 percent) reduction in the probability that the threat occurring will result in a larger IMV with little added resource protection.

Treatment Costs

The user must input the costs of recommended treatments separately for each VAR-threat association. This allows the VAR Calculation Tool to complete a discrete treatment justification for each Map Zone. Sources for current treatment costs vary by treatment. Most road and trail treatments costs can be provided by the area engineer. The costs of other treatments, such as hillslope and channel treatments, can be obtained for BAERCAT (Napper 2006), from the suppliers and service contractors who would be hired to apply the treatments if funding is approved.

Each Map Zone is reviewed independently and each treatment recommendation within a Map Zone requires a separate justification and decision. Some analyses may be very straight forward, especially where a high value asset can be protected using an inexpensive, highly effective treatment. For example, a water supply intake system serving a federal fish hatchery on public lands has intake filters valued at $500,000 that would have to be replaced if contaminated by ash and sediment-laden river water. It is expected, given the common autumn rainfall patterns, that the probability of this threat occurring is nearly 100 percent. A rainfall and flood warning system costing $15,000 will permit managers, with 90 percent chance of success,

Erosion Risk Management Tool: Mulch (0.5 ton / ac)

Bitterroot Valley MT +
sandy loam; 20% rock; 10%, 40%,20% slope; 800 ft; high soil burn severity
[Run ID wepp-16558]

Sediment delivery (ton / ac)	Percent 1st year
1.22	17.95
1.2	19.35
1.18	
1.16	
1.12	
1.06	19.46
1.06	
1.04	
1.01	
0.99	
0.95	
0.92	19.91
0.85	

Erosion Risk Management Tool: Mulch (1 ton / ac)

Bitterroot Valley MT +
sandy loam; 20% rock; 10%, 40%,20% slope; 800 ft; high soil burn severity
[Run ID wepp-16558]

Sediment delivery (ton / ac)	Percent 1st year
1.22	11.97
1.2	13.77
1.18	
1.16	
1.12	
1.06	13.88
1.06	
1.04	
1.01	
0.99	
0.95	
0.92	14.04
0.85	

Erosion Risk Management Tool: Mulch (1.5 ton / ac)

Bitterroot Valley MT +
sandy loam; 20% rock; 10%, 40%,20% slope; 800 ft; high soil burn severity
[Run ID wepp-16558]

Sediment delivery (ton / ac)	Percent 1st year
1.22	11.21
1.2	13.07
1.18	
1.16	
1.12	
1.06	13.18
1.06	
1.04	
1.01	
0.99	
0.95	
0.92	13.28
0.85	

Erosion Risk Management Tool: Mulch (2 ton / ac)

Bitterroot Valley MT +
sandy loam; 20% rock; 10%, 40%,20% slope; 800 ft; high soil burn severity
[Run ID wepp-16558]

Sediment delivery (ton / ac)	Percent chance that sediment delivery will be exceeded					Permutation Event rank Spatial burn Soil class
	1st year	2nd year	3rd year	4th year	5th year	
1.22	10.46	12.63	15.76			5HLH2
1.2	12.38					20HHH1
1.18		12.93	16.33	9.51	4.06	5LLH2
1.16					4.56	10LLL2
1.12			17.26	10.64	5.88	10LHL1
1.06	12.49	13.03	17.36			75HLH5
1.06		13.12	17.45	10.73	5.97	75LLH5
1.04		13.92	18.95	12.23	7.32	20LLH2
1.01			13.36	8.63		10HLL1
0.99		15.38	19.89	14.48	9.94	10LLH1
0.95			21.39	15.98	11.29	20LHL2
0.92	12.51	15.68	21.95	16.54		5HHL2
0.85					11.34	20LLL4

Figure 4. The truncated Sediment yield—probability of exceedance table (accessed through ERMiT output window) for each of the four mulching rates laid out to show the sediment delivery and probability of exceedance in the first year after the fire. The probability of exceeding the 1 t ac^{-1} tolerable sediment yield in the first post-fire year is circled on the table for each of the four mulching rates.

to shut the intake valves, divert the water, and protect the filters. The B/C calculation works out as:

$$B/C = (\$500{,}000 * 0.90)/\$15{,}000 = 30$$

Clearly this treatment is economically justified.

On the other hand, a historic fur traders' camp could be washed away if a low-probability (10 percent) flood event were to occur. A proposed hydro-mulching treatment costing $150,000 is expected to decrease the probability of a damaging flood to 5 percent. The IMV calculation yields:

$$IMV = \$150{,}000/0.05 = \$3{,}000{,}000$$

This is a very large IMV for a single, culturally significant but not unique, structure and the BAER team would likely not recommend this treatment be applied. They may seek a less expensive (albeit, less effective) treatment or decide that no treatment is the most justified. However, a B/C ratio less than 1 or a high IMV does not necessarily mean treatment should not occur, especially if the resource has a high value making any loss unacceptable. Under such circumstances, protection of the resource may be justifiable even if the cost of the protection is high. The VAR Calculation Tool does not make this judgment. It is simply a vehicle that describes the economic considerations of the BAER treatment decisions.

Using the VAR Calculation Tool

Once the input parameters are available, the VAR Calculation Tool can be used to calculate the B/C ratios and/or the IMV of the identified VAR and to organize and summarize the justification for recommended treatment expenditures.

This section explains how to use the VAR Calculation Tool. To get the most out of this section, we recommend you open the tool on the accompanying CD. The VAR Calculation Tool, written as an MS Excel spreadsheet, consists of four components: 1) the *Welcome* page or tab with instructions and background information; 2) the *VAR Area Map worksheet* page (second tab); 3) 10 *Map Zone* worksheets; and 4) a final *Summary* worksheet where the results of Map Zone worksheets are tabulated.

Welcome Page

The Welcome Page provides links to four instruction and support pages for the VAR Calculation Tool:

- *Introduction*—describes the risk-based assessment supported by the VAR Calculation Tool and differences in valuation methods used for market and non-market VAR.

- *Tool Use Preparation*—describes the information needed as input to the VAR Calculation Tool.

- *Structure and Use*—outlines the VAR valuation framework and how the calculations are done for the different categories of VAR. It also describes how the VAR Calculation Tool processes the user inputs on each Map Zone page and transfers totals to the summary page.

- *Definitions*—provides word definitions, particularly economic terms, that may not be common knowledge for all users.

The user can navigate to each section by clicking on the rectangular buttons. Return to the Welcome Page view by clicking the "CLEAR ALL" button or selecting the Welcome tab on the bottom of each spreadsheet.

> **Editing the VAR Calculation Tool:** This version of the VAR Calculation Tool has all pages locked for editing. However, the locks are not password protected and experienced users may release edit protections and make changes. The VAR Calculation Tool has two limits—only three VAR items per VAR category can be included on each Map Zone worksheet and only 10 Map Zones can be summarized. If Map Zone worksheets are added, corresponding changes must be made to the Summary sheets and cell reference formulas updated. Users who release edit protections and make changes assume responsibility for the calculation changes that may result.

USDA Forest Service RMRS-GTR-205. 2007.

Gash Creek Fire Example

To illustrate use of the VAR Calculation Tool to assess values-at-risk, we provide a scenario based on the 2006 Gash Creek Fire in the Bitterroot Valley, Montana. We changed some details and contrived scenarios to present the four types of VAR valuation processes (life and safety; market VAR only; non-market VAR only; and mixed market and non-market VAR) as well as the use of ERMiT to determine the expected probabilities of erosion occurring before and after treatments. We use the example to summarize the preparation steps, illustrate data entry into the VAR Calculation Tool, and interpret the output from the VAR Calculation Tool. We first describe the steps, give examples for each of the four evaluation categories, and then summarize all results in a separate section.

Gash Creek Fire Information

The 8,200 acre Gash Creek Fire burned in steep terrain along the east face of the Bitterroot Mountains, the west side of the Bitterroot Valley, on land primarily under Forest Service jurisdiction. Fires burned across a vegetation gradient from lower elevation dry forests through upper elevation cold, moist forest types. Burn severity was predominately low to moderate with several concentrated areas of high severity burn.

Preparation for VAR Valuation Within the BAER Process

At the first BAER team meeting, members of the team identified an initial list of VAR using current maps, GIS, and local area knowledge. A BARC map was available as a first assessment of burn severity and potential sources of post-fire threats. The initial VAR list included: life and safety of residents due to increased flooding potential, access to, and safety along, road and trail systems; stream crossings throughout the road network, including areas within and downstream of the burned area; critical aquatic habitat; and populations of rare and sensitive native plants. The BAER team added these identified VAR to the BARC map to focus field assessments. Because the trout habitat was downstream of two watersheds that were designated 20 percent (220 ac) high burn severity and 25 percent (280 ac) moderate burn severity, these slopes were field checked for soil burn severity. The BAER team determined that 1) nearly all of the BARC map high burn severity areas had high soil burn severity and 2) about half of the BARC map moderate burn severity hillslopes had large patches of moderate to high soil burn severity with little ground cover and more than 50 percent water repellent soils. The remainder of the moderate burn severity area had less severely impacted soil (more cover and little to no water repellency). Thus, only 150 acres of the BARC map moderate burn severity within these watersheds were a runoff-erosion threat to the identified VAR (several road culvert stream crossings and the trout habitat).

The BAER team identified four VAR-threat associations and mapped them as Map Zones A through D. The team completed descriptions of VAR and analyses of associated threats (for example, probabilities of occurrence with and without treatment). Mid-way through the BAER assessment process, the team contacted forest engineers and other sources to obtain the dollar value of identified market VAR. The team then designed and documented treatment plans with associated costs.

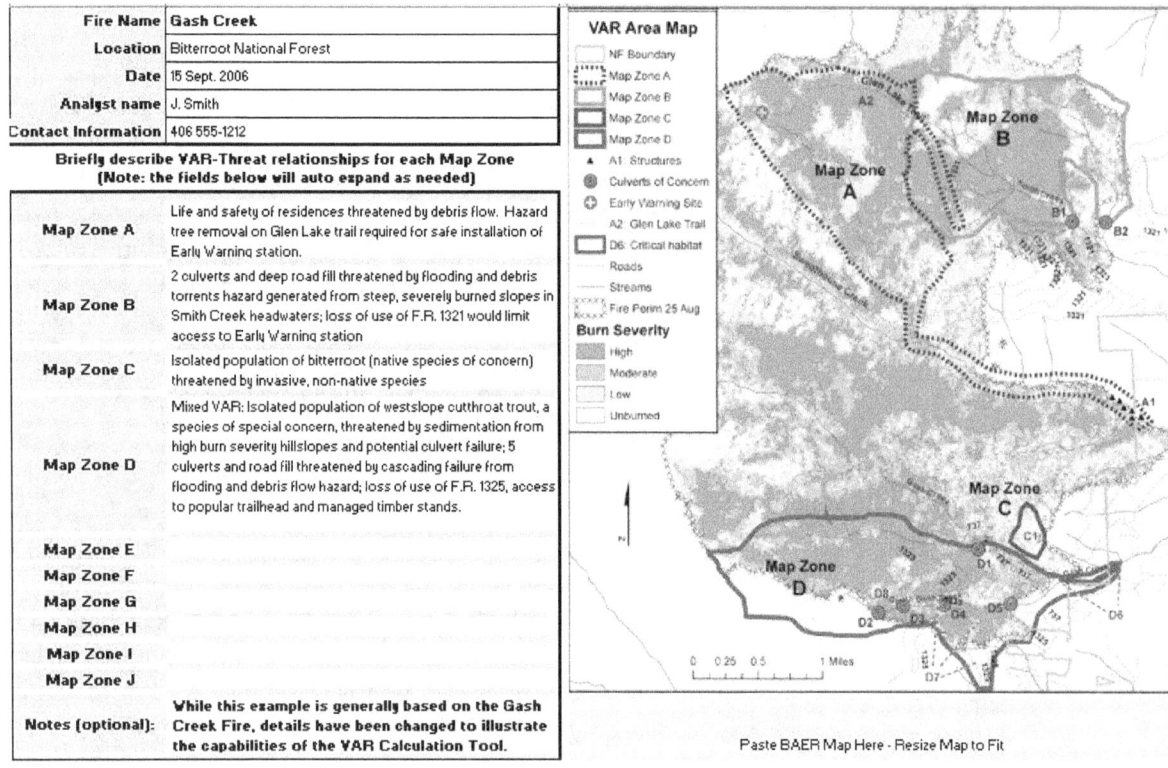

Figure 5. VAR Area Map worksheet from the VAR Calculation Tool for the Gash Creek example.

VAR Area Map Page

The VAR Area Map page includes the VAR Area Map (prepared earlier by the team; fig. 1) and a comment section that together provide an overview of the identified VAR (fig. 5). For the Gash Creek Fire, the team GIS specialist worked with resource specialists to compile a VAR Area Map and comment worksheet that showed the Map Zones of identified VAR-threat associations. They then copied and pasted the VAR Area Map into the designated space on the VAR Area Map page and resized as necessary. This can also be done by hand using hard copy maps. Next, the team completed the information box in the upper left corner of the VAR Area Map page. For each Map Zone, the team briefly summarized VAR-threat associations and added clarifying comments or notes as necessary.

Map Zone Worksheets

Ten individual worksheets, labeled Map Zone A through J, are used to independently evaluate the set of values-at-risk, threats, and treatments within each Map Zone. Map Zone worksheets are formatted in three sections: 1) Values-at-Risk, 2) Treatment Description, and 3) VAR Calculation Results (figs. 6 through 9).

To complete the Map Zone Worksheets, the Gash Creek Fire BAER Team first entered information into *white* cells as necessary to describe and compute the valuation of the values-at-risk (VAR) within the Map Zone and associated each VAR to a Map Link Number (figs. 6 through 9). They listed VARs by category (Life and Safety; Non-market VAR Cultural; Non-market VAR Ecological; Market VAR Direct; and Market VAR Loss of Use).

Note that any one Map Zone may not have all VAR categories. The team then wrote a brief description of each VAR in the right column. At the bottom of the VAR section, they entered "Probability of experiencing loss with **no** treatment" (as a decimal—in other words, if there is a 50 percent probability that the threat will occur, the probability is entered as 0.5) and from the dropdown menu, selected the source of the probability value entered.

In the Map Zone Treatment Description section, the team briefly described the proposed treatments and listed the assigned Map Link Number for each treatment. They then entered the estimated treatment cost. For example, in Map Zone B (fig. 7), the total estimated cost for installing armored diversion dips and reinforcing culvert inlets was $8,405. Next, they estimated the "Probability of experiencing loss if treatment occurs" as a decimal (for example, in Map Zone B in fig. 7, the probability was 5 percent, so was entered as 0.05). Finally, they used the dropdown menu to select the source of the loss probability with treatment information.

Fire Name	Gash Creek
Location	Bitterroot National Forest
Date	15 Sept. 2006

EACH MAP ZONE REPRESENTS A SYSTEM OF LINKED TREATMENTS AND ASSOCIATED VALUES AT RISK

MAP ZONE A - VALUES AT RISK (VAR)

Map link #	Life and Safety	Description
A1	Residence at risk from flooding	Downslope homes require early warning system in the event of hillslope failure
A2	Safe access for installation of system	Glen Lake trail needs hazard tree removal for safe installation of early warning system

PLEASE NOTE: IF PUBLIC SAFETY IS A FACTOR, B/C RATIO SHOULD NOT BE RELEVANT AND SHOULD STRICTLY BE AN ACCOUNTING EXERCISE

Map link #	Non-Market: Cultural Values	Description

Map link #	Non-Market: Ecological	Description

Map link #	Market Values: Direct	Description	Total
			$ -
			$ -
			$ -

Map link #	Market Values: Loss-of-Use	Description	Total
A2	Recreation value	Loss of recreation use along Glen Lake trail	$ -
			$ -
			$ -

Probability of experiencing the loss with no treatment (enter as decimal)	0.30
Source of loss probability with no treatment: Expert Opinion	
Market Resource Value	$ -

TREATMENT DESCRIPTION

Map link #	Proposed treatment	Total
A1	Install early warning system	$ 5,200
A2	Hazard tree removal along Glen Lake trail	$ 1,943
		$ -

Probability of experiencing loss if treatment occurs (enter as decimal)	0.00
Source of loss probability with treatment: Expert Opinion	
Total Treatment Cost	$ 7,143

VAR CALCULATION RESULTS

REDUCTION IN PROBABILITY OF LOSS	0.30
EXPECTED BENEFIT OF TREATMENT	$ -
Expected Benefit/Cost ratio of treatment for market resources only (economically justified if > 1.0)	
IMPLIED MINIMUM VALUE OF PROTECTING NON-MARKET RESOURCE VALUES	$ -

| Comments | Life and safety are primary concern - No further economic analysis was conducted |

Figure 6. Map Zone A worksheet from the VAR Calculation Tool with details for the Gash Creek Fire example.

Fire Name	Gash Creek		
Location	Bitterroot National Forest		
Date	15 Sept. 2006		

EACH MAP ZONE REPRESENTS A SYSTEM OF LINKED TREATMENTS AND ASSOCIATED VALUES AT RISK

MAP ZONE B - VALUES AT RISK (VAR)

Map link #	Life and Safety	Description	

PLEASE NOTE: IF PUBLIC SAFETY IS A FACTOR, B/C RATIO SHOULD NOT BE RELEVANT AND SHOULD STRICTLY BE AN ACCOUNTING EXERCISE

Map link #	Non-Market: Cultural Values	Description	

Map link #	Non-Market: Ecological	Description	

Map link #	Market Values: Direct	Description	Total
B1,B2	Culverts and fill along Forest Rd 1321	Large culverts, deep fill along heavy traffic road	$ 58,883
			$ -
			$ -

Map link #	Market Values: Loss-of-Use	Description	
			$ -
			$ -
			$ -

Probability of experiencing the loss with no treatment (enter as decimal)	0.10
Source of loss probability with no treatment: Expert Opinion	
Market Resource Value	$ 58,883

TREATMENT DESCRIPTION

Map link #	Proposed treatment	Total
B1,B2	Install armored diversion dips, reinforce culvert inlets	$ 8,405
		$ -
		$ -

Probability of experiencing loss if treatment occurs (enter as decimal)	0.05
Source of loss probability with treatment: Expert Opinion	
Total Treatment Cost	$ 8,405

VAR CALCULATION RESULTS

REDUCTION IN PROBABILITY OF LOSS	0.05
EXPECTED BENEFIT OF TREATMENT	$ 2,944
Expected Benefit/Cost ratio of treatment for market resources only (economically justified if > 1.0)	0.35
IMPLIED MINIMUM VALUE OF PROTECTING NON-MARKET RESOURCE VALUES	$ -

Comments	B/C ratio of 0.35 indicates treatment is not economically justified

Figure 7. Map Zone B worksheet from the VAR Calculation Tool with details for the Gash Creek Fire example.

There are occasions when a single treatment may provide protection to more than one VAR and probabilities of loss with and without treatment will differ for each identified threat-VAR association. For example, a hillslope erosion mitigation treatment may reduce the probability of damage to a stream quality VAR by reducing sedimentation and the same treatment may reduce the probability of damage to roads and culverts by reducing runoff and peak flows. The probabilities associated with damaging hillslope erosion may be different than the probabilities associated with damaging runoff and peak flows (see Map Zone D discussion). The current version of the VAR Calculation Tool can only apply a single set of treatment effectiveness probabilities to generate benefit-cost ratio and/or IMV. When two or more sets of probabilities can be applied to a treatment, assessment teams may have to decide how best to represent the probabilities of the loss occurring with and without treatment. This could be done by: 1) combining the different probabilities and using "average" or "weighted average" probabilities on the Map Zone worksheet; 2) choosing one set of probabilities over the others because one threat is more likely to occur or is the primary threat under consideration; and 3) running each VAR-threat-treatment combination on a separate Map Zone worksheet to determine if any one set clearly justifies the treatment.

For Map Zone A, **life and safety** are at risk (fig. 6). Treatment justification is established by providing a reasonable description of how prevailing post-fire conditions might lead to death or injury, and neither a benefit-cost ratio nor IMV calculation is needed. A treatment plan and cost estimate will be completed, and probabilities of loss with and without treatment should still be considered as a practical check on the choice and magnitude of proposed treatments.

In the Gash Creek Fire example, an early warning system to detect a debris torrent that could damage downstream residences is required to warn affected residents of an impending event (this scenario is contrived for this illustration). The Glen Lake trail provides the access route to install and maintain the required system and additionally, is an important recreational route. Following the fire, more than 200 downed stems crossed the trail and 35 adjacent snags prohibited safe worker access to install the recommended BAER treatment. The probabilities of loss with and without treatment were based upon the anticipated need for the early warning system. The treatment, installing the early warning system, was expected to be completely effective, providing sufficient warning in the event of a land movement event. Hazard tree removal is required so that those installing the early warning system can safely conduct their work. Probability of loss without treatment was estimated at 30 percent, reduced to 0 percent with treatment (fig. 6).

For Map Zone B, where only market VAR are at risk, the treatment justification is determined using a benefit-cost (B/C) ratio (fig. 7). Market VAR valuations require determination of the dollar value lost if the associated threat materializes (in other words, the cost to repair or replace the VAR if it were damaged or lost), the cost of treatment, and the probability that the proposed treatment will be successful. The "Benefit" (the expected value of the reduction in damage or loss to the VAR defined as market value times the reduction in the likelihood of loss with treatment) is compared to the "Cost" (the dollar expense of the proposed treatments).

In the Gash Creek Fire BAER assessment, the team identified two major culverts and the associated road surfaces along a forest road (fig. 5, Map Zone B, points B1 and B2) as VAR threatened by potential flooding and debris-laden flows from the high severely burned slopes above the road. Field observations verified culvert locations and conditions relative to burn severity and terrain. However, given the size of the culverts (60 inches) and the well-armored installations, it was determined that only an extreme event would potentially damage or destroy these VAR. A forest engineer provided cost estimates to repair the culverts and road surfaces as well as the costs of installing armored diversion dips to fortify water crossings to minimize flood impacts. Consulting with the engineers, the hydrologist estimated a 10 percent probability of loss without treatment, which would be reduced to 5 percent with treatments in place. The potential **loss of use** of the road (another market VAR) was acknowledged but the monetary value was not included due to lack of information (fig. 7).

For Map Zone C, the team found only **non-market VAR** and therefore used Implied Minimum Value (IMV) for valuation (fig. 8). No dollar value is directly assigned to the non-market VAR; instead an IMV amount is applied based on the cost of treatment adjusted for the reduction in the probability of loss averted by the treatment. The IMV is used to make a judgment as to the economic justification of the proposed treatment.

The VAR identified in Map Zone C was a population of rare perennial bitterroot plants. Bitterroot is the namesake of the valley, the Montana State flower, and culturally significant to native peoples. Once abundant, it is now uncommon, particularly on the west side of the valley. Invasive plants, the identified threat associated with the VAR, were expected to spread and probably out-compete the bitterroots if the invasive plants were not suppressed until the bitterroots were re-established the following spring. Given that invasive weeds were already established along a road above the impacted area, the BAER team botanist estimated that there was a 50 percent probability that invasive plants would out-compete bitterroots in the first post-fire growing season. Seeding with annual grasses, including ground-based hydromulch treatments near the road (at a cost of $29,700) was expected to be an effective treatment that would reduce the probability of bitterroot plant loss to 5 percent (fig. 8). The IMV resulting from the calculation was

Fire Name	Gash Creek			
Location	Bitterroot National Forest			
Date	15 Sept. 2006			
EACH MAP ZONE REPRESENTS A SYSTEM OF LINKED TREATMENTS AND ASSOCIATED VALUES AT RISK				
MAP ZONE C - VALUES AT RISK (VAR)				
Map link #	**Life and Safety**	**Description**		
PLEASE NOTE: IF PUBLIC SAFETY IS A FACTOR, B/C RATIO SHOULD NOT BE RELEVANT AND SHOULD STRICTLY BE AN ACCOUNTING EXERCISE				
Map link #	**Non-Market: Cultural Values**	**Description**		
C1	bitterroot plants	hertiage value to native peoples, MT state flower		
Map link #	**Non-Market: Ecological**	**Description**		
C1	bitterroot plants	populations diminished throughout region		
Map link #	**Market Values: Direct**	**Description**	**Total**	
			$	-
			$	-
			$	-
Map link #	**Market Values: Loss-of-Use**	**Description**		
			$	-
			$	-
			$	-
Probability of experiencing the loss with no treatment (enter as decimal)				0.50
Source of loss probability with no treatment:		Expert Opinion		
		Market Resource Value	$	-
TREATMENT DESCRIPTION				
Map link #	**Proposed treatment**		**Total**	
C1	seeding with annual grasses and monitoring		$	29,700
			$	-
			$	-
Probability of experiencing loss if treatment occurs (enter as decimal)				0.10
Source of loss probability with treatment:		Expert Opinion		
		Total Treatment Cost	$	29,700
VAR CALCULATION RESULTS				
REDUCTION IN PROBABILITY OF LOSS				0.40
EXPECTED BENEFIT OF TREATMENT			$	-
Expected Benefit/Cost ratio of treatment for market resources only (economically justified if > 1.0)				
IMPLIED MINIMUM VALUE OF PROTECTING NON-MARKET RESOURCE VALUES			$	74,250
Comments	Expert opinion of probability of loss provided by local forest botantist;			

Figure 8. Map Zone C worksheet from the VAR Calculation Tool with details for the Gash Creek Fire example.

$74,250. [Note: In this case, the VAR-threat association was located in an area of low burn severity—an area that would typically get little attention from a BAER team. The threat to bitterroots, which was not initially expected, was only determined by field observation.]

For Map Zone D, the team identified a combination of **market and non-market VAR**, which is typical of many burned areas (fig. 9). Identified VAR included road surfaces and culverts and a population of a sensitive aquatic species. The B/C ratio for the market VAR is less than 1.0. Thus, treatments are not economically justified without consideration of the IMV of the non-market ecological VAR.

Map Zone D consists of two adjacent, elongated watersheds. The larger is drained by South Gash Creek and the second is an unnamed tributary of Gash Creek. Identified VAR include two actively used forest roads along which five culverts are located (four in sequence along South Gash Creek and one near the mouth of the unnamed tributary; fig. 5, Map Zone D, points D1 to D5). In addition, an identified non-market VAR is an isolated population of westslope cutthroat trout, a species of special concern, located in a reach of Gash Creek below the confluence with South Gash Creek (fig. 5, Map Zone D, point D6). The culverts and road crowns are at-risk of damage from runoff (the associated threat) that would exceed culvert capacity. The hydrologist (in consultation with the forest engineer) predicted that there

Figure 9. Map Zone D worksheet from the VAR Calculation Tool with details for the Gash Creek Fire example.

was a 20 percent chance that a rainfall event would generate enough run-off to exceed culvert capacity. This runoff event would not only damage the roads and culverts, but would likely generate channel-scouring flooding with sediment- and debris-laden flows that would impact the downstream trout habitat. The hydrologist (in consultation with the fisheries biologist) determined that the trout population would be damaged beyond recovery by hillslope sediment yields in excess of 1.0 t ac^{-1} from the contributing area above the trout habitat. Hillslope sediment yields of this magnitude could destroy the trout population which, due to habitat fragmentation and diversions, may not repopulate the reach.

The ERMiT model predicted a 40 percent occurrence probability that the sediment yield from the high soil burn severity hillslopes would exceed 1 t ac^{-1} for a single rain event in the first year after the fire (fig. 10). This sediment would be in addition to the sediment that might result from any road crossing failures. The same ERMiT run also predicted aerial application of straw mulch at 1 t ac^{-1} rate would reduce the probability of exceeding 1 t ac^{-1} event sediment yield to 6 percent (fig. 11).

The hillslope straw mulch treatment would likely reduce the runoff peak flows and thus reduce the risk of exceeding culvert capacities. The hydrologist estimated, using professional judgment and runoff predictions from hydrological models, that the proposed hillslope treatment would reduce the probability of damage to the culverts and the road (market VAR) from 20 percent to 5 percent. Reduced probability of road and culvert damage also reduces the likelihood of additional sediment (beyond the hillslope sediment predicted by ERMiT) from entering the trout habitat (non-market VAR). However, the current version of the VAR Calculation Tool can only apply a single set of treatment effectiveness probabilities to generate a B/C ratio and/or IMV. In this scenario, the assessment team has two sets of probabilities related to the aerial straw mulch treatment—the probability that hillslope sediment yield will exceed the tolerable limit (40 percent without treatment reduced to 6 percent with treatment) and the probability that runoff will damage culverts and roads (20 percent without treatment reduced to 5 percent with treatment). The assessment team used the treatment effectiveness probabilities associated with hillslope sediment yield that were generated from ERMiT. The rationale for this example decision included: 1) the cost of the aerial straw treatment far exceeds the cost of culvert replacement (a market VAR) and the B/C ratio is much less than 1.0; 2) the aerial straw mulch treatment justification will depend on the implied minimum value (IMV) of the trout habitat (non-market VAR); 3) exceeding the tolerable hillslope sediment yield is the more likely threat; and 4) the ERMiT values for treatment effectiveness are based on field measurements and the treatment effects on runoff were based on several estimated parameter values being used in runoff equations.

In the final section of each Map Zone Worksheet Page in the VAR Calculation Results section, *orange* cells will fill automatically and results will transfer to the Summary page (fig. 12; Appendix A shows calculation methods applied by the VAR Calculation Tool). For the IMV calculation to occur, entries must be made in the non-market VAR sections, as well as in the treatment cost, probability of experiencing loss with no treatment, and probability of experiencing loss if treatment occurs sections. If the map zone includes both market and non-market values, the IMV will be calculated only if the market value B/C ratio is less than one.

Erosion Risk Management Tool: Untreated

Figure 10. The ERMiT Sediment Yield—probabilities of exceedance table (accessed from the ERMiT output webpage) showing a 40 percent occurrence probability for single event sediment yield that will exceed 1 ton ac[-1] from a modeled untreated hillslope.

STEVENSVILLE MT +
sandy loam; 30% rock; 25%, 40%,20% slope; 1000 ft; high soil burn severity
[Run ID wepp-20171]

Sediment delivery (ton / ac)	Percent chance that sediment delivery will be exceeded					Permutation Event rank Spatial burn Soil class
	1st year	2nd year	3rd year	4th year	5th year	
24.92	1.2					20HHH5
22.08	1.27					10HHH5
17.93	1.35					5HHH5
			Table rows removed			
1.18	36.9	21.21				5LHH1
1.15		22.52	8.39	4.76	2.79	50LLH4
1.08	37.28					75HHH5
1.08		23.08	8.95	5.33	3.29	10LLH2
1.07	38.92	24.39	9.02			50HLH4
1.05	39.38	24.95	9.58			10HLH2
0.95		25.02	9.65	5.39	3.36	50LLH5
0.92		26.39	10.89	5.94	3.43	50LLH3
0.9	42.68	27.77	12.13			50HLH3

Erosion Risk Management Tool: Mulch (1 ton / ac)

STEVENSVILLE MT +
sandy loam; 30% rock; 25%, 40%,20% slope; 1000 ft; high soil burn severity
[Run ID wepp-20171]

Sediment delivery (ton / ac)	Percent chance that sediment delivery will be exceeded					Permutation Event rank Spatial burn Soil class
	1st year	2nd year	3rd year	4th year	5th year	
24.92	1.02					20HHH5
22.08	1.03					10HHH5
17.93	1.03					5HHH5
			Table rows removed			
1.18	6.14	8.16				5LHH1
1.15		8.23	8.39	4.76	2.79	50LLH4
1.08	6.18					75HHH5
1.08		8.61	8.95	5.33	3.29	10LLH2
1.07	6.26	8.67	9.02			50HLH4
1.05	6.42	9.05	9.58			10HLH2
0.95		9.12	9.65	5.39	3.36	50LLH5
0.92		9.67	10.89	5.94	3.43	50LLH3
0.9	6.5	10.22	12.13			50HLH3

Figure 11. The ERMiT Sediment Yield—probabilities of exceedance table (accessed from the ERMiT output webpage) showing a 6 percent occurrence probability for single event sediment yield that will exceed 1 ton ac[-1] from a modeled hillslope treated with 1 ton ac[-1] aerial straw mulch.

SUMMARY

Total Treatment Cost	$	202,748
Expected Benefit of Treatment	$	40,011
Implied Minimum Value (IMV)	$	428,466

MAP ZONE A

Value Type	Value at Risk	Implied Value and/or Benefit Cost
Life and Safety	Yes	
Non-Market: Cultural Values	No	
Non-Market: Ecological Values	No	
Market Values: Direct	No	
Market Values: Loss of Use	Yes	$ -
Total Market Resource Value		$ -
Proposed Treatment		$ 7,143
Reduction in Probability of Loss		0.30
Expected Benefit of Treatment		$ -
Exp B/C Ratio of Treatment for Market Resources Only		
Implied Minimum Value (IMV) of Protecting Non-Market Resource Values		$ -

MAP ZONE B

Value Type	Value at Risk	Implied Value and/or Benefit Cost
Life and Safety	No	
Non-Market: Cultural Values	No	
Non-Market: Ecological Values	No	
Market Values: Direct	Yes	$ 58,883
Market Values: Loss of Use	No	$ -
Total Market Resource Value		$ 58,883
Proposed Treatment		$ 8,405
Reduction in Probability of Loss		0.05
Expected Benefit of Treatment		$ 2,944
Exp B/C Ratio of Treatment for Market Resources Only		0.35
Implied Minimum Value (IMV) of Protecting Non-Market Resource Values		

MAP ZONE C

Value Type	Value at Risk	Implied Value and/or Benefit Cost
Life and Safety	No	
Non-Market: Cultural Values	Yes	
Non-Market: Ecological Values	Yes	
Market Values: Direct	No	$ -
Market Values: Loss of Use	No	$ -
Total Market Resource Value		$ -
Proposed Treatment		$ 29,700
Reduction in Probability of Loss		0.40
Expected Benefit of Treatment		$ -
Exp B/C Ratio of Treatment for Market Resources Only		
Implied Minimum Value (IMV) of Protecting Non-Market Resource Values		$ 74,250

MAP ZONE D

Value Type	Value at Risk	Implied Value and/or Benefit Cost
Life and Safety	No	
Non-Market: Cultural Values	No	
Non-Market: Ecological Values	Yes	
Market Values: Direct	Yes	$ 59,020
Market Values: Loss of Use	Yes	$ 50,000
Total Market Resource Value		$ 109,020
Proposed Treatment		$ 157,500
Reduction in Probability of Loss		0.34
Expected Benefit of Treatment		$ 37,067
Exp B/C Ratio of Treatment for Market Resources Only		0.24
Implied Minimum Value (IMV) of Protecting Non-Market Resource Values		$ 354,215

Figure 12. VAR Calculation Tool Summary Worksheet for the Gash Creek example.

We have provided the user a brief review of literature sources for determining non-market values. At the bottom of the Map Zone Worksheets is a button, "View Literature." The literature is grouped into five categories: property, soil productivity, threatened and endangered (T&E) species, water quality, and wildlife. We do not recommend that these sources be used to identify a monetary price for non-market values—the IMV approach to valuation of non-market VAR is the recommended process. However, the literature may provide some valuation comparisons that would be useful to some BAER teams. The more similar the described VAR is to the resource evaluated in the literature, the more appropriate the comparison. If literature exists that provides estimates of the dollar value of a non-market resource that is similar to the evaluated BAER resource in terms of physical characteristics and setting, a calculated IMV that is substantially lower than the literature estimate provides added justification for the proposed treatment.

Summary Page

Key values from each Map Zone are automatically transferred to the Summary Worksheet (fig. 12). These include: 1) Value Types assessed (Life & Safety, Non-market, and/or Market values),

2) Total Market Resource Value, 3) Proposed Treatment Costs, 4) Reduction in the Probability of Loss, 5) Expected Benefit of Treatment, 6) Expected B/C Ratio for Market Resources, and 7) IMV for Non-market Resources. The entire Summary Page is "view-only"—no changes to inputs are directly made on this page. Instead, informed by review and comparison across Map Zones, the user can return to individual Map Zone worksheets as necessary to evaluate VAR, probabilities, and treatment components. Where data have been entered within a VAR category on the individual Map Zone worksheets, the "Value-at-Risk" cell on the Summary page will show "Yes." Transferred values include the sum of market values and treatment costs, loss probability values, B/C ratio for market resources, and the IMV calculations for non-market resources. The summary of each Map Zone should be reviewed independently to ensure that the cost to protect low value resources is not subsidized by high value resources in another Map Zone.

The VAR Calculation Tool Summary Page may be used to summarize and report total proposed treatment costs and estimated outcomes in terms of expected market values protected and the IMV associated with the non-market values protected for an entire BAER incident. At the top of the Summary Worksheet (fig. 12), three values are tallied for the whole assessment: 1) Total Treatment Cost; 2) Expected Benefit of Treatment, and 3) Implied Minimum Value. For the Gash Creek VAR analysis, treatments totaling $202,748 were proposed to protect market resources with expected benefit of treatments totaling $40,011 and an IMV of $428,466 for non-market resources (top of fig. 12). The relatively low expected market benefits value indicates that the primary justification for the selected treatments is based on highly valued non-market VAR values (values exceed the $428,466 calculated IMV). Beyond these general observations, summary values alone do not provide economic justification for proposed treatments and individual Map Zones need to be evaluated on their own merit.

Summary of Map Zone A—The two value types entered into the Map Zone A worksheet transferred automatically to the corresponding summary box, Life and Safety and Market Values: Loss of Use (fig. 12). Recall that Life and Safety are documented as the primary concern. Therefore, Loss of Use, while noted and described, is not quantified. Assuming the threat to Life and Safety is mapped and documented, the VAR analysis is complete and the proposed treatment at a cost of $7,143 is justified. However attention should be paid to the Reduction on Probability of Loss. In this example, treatment is expected to eliminate risk, reducing risk from 30 percent to 0 percent (fig. 6). Treatments with low threat reduction potential would indicate that proposed treatments do not provide substantial mitigation of the threat(s) to life and safety and should be carefully reviewed.

Summary of Map Zone B—The direct market value ($58,883) of the road infrastructures threatened by potential flooding and debris-laden flows is listed in the Map Zone B block of the Summary worksheet (fig. 12). Proposed treatments, at a cost of $8,405, provide a minimal reduction (5 percent) in the probability of loss. Thus, the expected benefit of treatment is reduced to $2,944, which yields a B/C ratio of 0.35, well below the threshold of economic justification of B/C ratio > 1.0. In this case, the probability of a destructive event (threat) occurring without treatment was low (10 percent, fig. 7) and treatment would only modestly mitigate the outcome. Consequently, the BAER team would likely determine that the proposed treatment for Map Zone B is not economically justified and would not request funding for the treatment.

Summary of Map Zone C—Calculations indicate that the treatments proposed at a cost of $29,700 to control the expected spread of noxious weeds would reduce the probability of loss by 40 percent (fig. 12). Therefore, the IMV of protecting the rare bitterroot plants is $74,250. The BAER team must judge if the ecological and cultural value of maintaining the bitterroot plants in this area exceeds the IMV of $74,250 and thus is worth the expenditure of $29,700 in public funds to conduct this treatment.

Summary of Map Zone D—Both market and non-market VAR are identified in Map Zone D and the B/C ratio for the market VAR of 0.2 is very low (fig. 9). Based on protection of market VAR alone, treatments are not economically justified. However, an IMV of $354,215 is calculated for the non-market ecological VAR—namely, the aquatic habitat for the protected trout species (fig. 9). As with Map Zone C, the BAER team must judge if the ecological value of protecting the trout habitat exceeds the IMV of $354,215. If so, the investment of $157,500 of public funds to conduct the treatment is justified. If not, the treatment should not occur.

Management Implications

Procedures and Planning for Effective VAR Calculation Tool Use

Our survey of BAER personnel revealed that the preparations necessary for using the VAR Calculation Tool are, at some level, already implemented by most experienced BAER leaders and teams. Two levels of preparation—one in the pre-fire season and one in the days just prior to convening a BAER team—will likely make the use of the VAR Calculation Tool more effective. These preparations will improve access to needed data and improve GIS support during the BAER assessment.

In areas where fires requiring BAER assessments are likely to occur, commonly required data for post-fire assessments can be compiled and made easily accessible prior to the start of the fire season. Non-spatial support data, including *local* monetary costs of frequently encountered market VAR (for example, roads, picnic area facilities, grazing leases) and regularly used treatments (for example, straw mulching, road grading, culvert installation), can be cataloged for easy access by potential BAER teams. In addition, local GIS data can be obtained and organized. Thus, when a fire occurs, the BAER team can have immediate access to a base map and resource data libraries, including topographic maps, jurisdictions, roads, Digital Elevation Models (DEMs) and derivatives, vegetation layers, hydrologic features, infrastructure and facilities, range and riparian areas, soils and geology, wildlife habitat, and special areas. Planning discussions with GIS personnel can determine the most commonly used data layers and establish standard BAER templates for common map features.

A second type of preparation also can facilitate BAER assessment with the VAR Calculation Tool. Prior to the first meeting of a BAER team, the available maps and data layers discussed above can be opened and updated with current fire information. This provides a detailed and relevant map for use at the initial BAER meeting. With a base map in place and many of the relevant VAR already identified and located, the BAER team can more quickly assess the current event and plan the assessment process.

Support for Post-fire Treatment Decisions and Funding Requests

Using the VAR Calculation Tool as part of the treatment decision-making processes requires 1) an understanding of how the tool calculates the B/C ratio of market VAR and the IMV of non-market VAR and 2) iterative use of the tool to evaluate the economic advantages of various treatment scenarios. The VAR Calculation Tool presents a logical and consistent VAR analysis report format that can be included in the BAER funding requests (DOI BAER ESR forms and USFS BAER 2500-8 forms) to justify treatment recommendations and facilitate review. We believe that implementing these tools will improve the economic justification of recommended treatments, provide a common framework for authorization and review of proposed treatments, and improve the defensibility of BAER assessments to agencies and individuals with financial oversight responsibilities.

References

Calkin, D.E.; Robichaud, P.R.; Jones, J.G. 2006. Pilot study: Improving BAER calculation of Values-at-Risk (JFSP 05-01-01-09). Final Report to Joint Fire Sciences Program. [Online]. Available: http://www.firescience.gov/projects/05-1-1-09/05-1-1-09_final_report.pdf [accessed 5 April 2007].

Finney, M. 2005. The challenge of quantitative risk analysis for wildland fire. Forest Ecology Management. 211: 97-108.

Hammond, C.; Hall, D.; Miller, S.; Swetik, P. 1992. Level I Stability Analysis (LISA) documentation for version 2.0. General Technical Report INT-285. Ogden, UT: U.S. Department of Agriculture, Forest Service, Intermountain Research Station. 190 p.

Napper, Carolyn. 2006. Burned Area Emergency Response Treatments Catalog. Technical Report. 0625 1801-SDTDC, Washington, D.C.: U.S. Department of Agriculture, Forest Service, National Technology & Development Program, Watershed, Soil, Air Management. 266 p. [Online]. available: http://www.fs.fed.us/eng/pubs/pdf/BAERCAT/lo_res/06251801L.pdf [accessed 24 April 2007].

Pigou, A.C. 1938. The economics of welfare. 4th ed. London: Macmillan.

Robichaud, Peter R.; Beyers, Jan L.; Neary, Daniel G. 2000. Evaluating the effectiveness of postfire rehabilitation treatments. Gen. Tech. Rep. RMRS-GTR-63, Fort Collins: U.S. Department of Agriculture, Forest Service, Rocky Mountain Research Station. 85 p.

Robichaud, P.R.; Elliot, W.J.; Pierson, F.B.; Hall, D.E.; Moffet, C.A. 2006. Erosion Risk Management Tool (ERMiT) Ver. 2006.01.18. Moscow, ID: U.S. Department of Agriculture, Forest Service, Rocky Mountain Research Station [Online]. Available: http://forest.moscowfsl.wsu.edu/fswepp/ [accessed 13 March 2007].

Robichaud, Peter R.; Elliot, William J.; Pierson, Fredreick B.; Hall, David E.; Moffet, Corey A.; Ashmun, Louise E. 2007. Erosion Risk Management Tool (ERMiT) user manual (version 2006.01.18). Gen. Tech. Rep. RMRS-GTR-188. Fort Collins, CO: U.S. Department of Agriculture, Forest Service, Rocky Mountain Research Station. 24 p.

Rosenberger, R.S.; Loomis, J.B. 2001. Benefit transfer of outdoor recreation use values: a technical document supporting the Forest Service Strategic Plan (2000 revision). Gen. Tech. Rep. RMRS-GTR-72. Fort Collins, CO: U.S. Department of Agriculture, Forest Service, Rocky Mountain Research Station. 59 p.

U.S. Department of Interior. 2004. Chapter 3 - Burned area emergency stabilization and rehabilitation. In: Departmental Manual, Public Lands, Part 620. Washington, D.C.: U.S. Department of Interior.

USDA Forest Service. 2004. Chapter 2523 - Watershed protection and management. In: Forest Service Manual. Washington, D.C: U.S. Department of Agriculture, Forest Service.

Venn, T.J.; Calkin, D.E. (2007). Challenges of socio-economically evaluating wildfire management in and adjacent to non-industrial private forestland in the western United States. In: Harrison, S.R., Bosch, A. and Herbohn, J.L. (eds.), Improving the Triple Bottom Line Returns from Small-scale Forestry. Proceedings from IUFRO Working Groups 3.08 Small-scale Forestry and 6.11.02 Forestry and Rural Development in Industrialized Countries, 17 to 21 June 2007, Ormoc City, the Philippines, The University of Queensland, Brisbane, pp. 383-396.

Appendix A—Calculations Within the VAR Calculation Tool

Depending on the user designation of the VAR-threat association being evaluated, the VAR Calculation Tool uses one of three calculation processes: 1) B/C ratio for market VAR only, 2) IMV for non-market VAR only, and 3) a hybrid of both B/C ratio and IMV for both market and non-market VAR.

Market values—Where all the identified VAR in a Map Zone are listed as market values, only the B/C ratio will be calculated for that Map Zone. The B/C ratio is the loss of market value of the resource if the threat occurs times the reduction in likelihood of experiencing the loss divided by treatment cost:

$$\text{B/C ratio} = \frac{\text{loss of value (\$)} \times (\text{Prob (loss without treatment)} - \text{Prob (losss with treatment)})}{\text{treatment cost (\$)}}$$

If, for example, the 1) forest roads and culverts at risk for failure due to flooding would require $28,000 to repair; 2) probability that flooding will occur without treatment is 90 percent; and 3) probability the flooding will occur with hillslope treatments (treatment cost=$16,000) in place is 30 percent, the calculation would be:

$$\text{B/C ratio} = \frac{\$28,000 \times (0.9\text{-}0.3)}{\$16,000} = 1.1$$

Thus, the treatment is economically justified. If the results for a given Map Zone are economically unfavorable, in other words the B/C ratio < 1.0, the proposed treatments should be reconsidered. If, in spite of the unfavorable B/C ratio, the BAER team believes a proposed treatment is needed, there may be some market VAR (such as loss of use) or non-market VAR (such as ecological values) that were not adequately considered. However, the user should be wary of manipulating the inputs to get a favorable B/C ratio for market VAR, as it defeats the purpose of using a B/C ratio for treatment decisions.

Non-market values—Where all of the identified VAR in a Map Zone are listed as non-market VAR, only the IMV will be calculated. IMV is based on the concept of break even analysis—what is the minimum value of a given resource so that the treatment expenditure is justified (in other words, B/C ratio =1.0)? IMV is calculated as the cost of the treatment divided by the reduction in the likelihood of experiencing the loss:

$$\text{IMV} = \left(\frac{\text{treatment cost (\$)}}{\text{Prob (loss occurring with no treatment)} - \text{Prob (loss occurring with treatment)}} \right)$$

The IMV approach does not result in a monetary value being assigned to the non-market VAR. Reducing the probability of loss to the described VAR should be justified at the IMV value. Considered judgment must be applied to determine if protection of a non-market VAR is worth at least the IMV and is a wise investment of public funds. If, for example, the 1) likelihood of experiencing loss of a population of bitterroot to invasive species is estimated to be 80 percent; 2) hand spraying invasive weeds and monitoring in the area will cost $5,000; and 3) probability of experiencing loss of the bitterroot population with the spray treatment is 50 percent, then the IMV of the bitterroot population is calculated as:

$$IMV = \frac{\$5,000}{0.8 - 0.5} = \$16,667$$

The decision of whether the treatment is justified is based on a determination of whether the presence of bitterroots in this Map Zone is worth at least $16,667. If so, the treatment is justified; if not, this treatment should not occur. A qualitative description of the potential resource damage or loss without treatment is needed to justify the BAER treatment funding request. Funding approval will depend on the reviewers' corroboration of the BAER team's judgment that the VAR valuation is equal to or greater than the IMV.

Both market and non-market values—When treatments are proposed to reduce the likelihood of losses to both market and non-market VAR within a given Map Zone, a hybrid approach is used. First, the B/C ratio is determined by examining the market VAR value change, reduction in the likelihood of loss, and the treatment costs without consideration of the non-market VAR. If the B/C ratio is greater than 1.0, the proposed treatments are justified and the non-market VAR need not be evaluated. If, however, the B/C ratio is less than 1.0, the value required to justify proposed treatments is then assigned to non-market VAR and interpreted through the calculated IMV. Determining if the treatments are economically justified is then the same as for non-market VAR alone. If, for example, water quality of a stream and a forest road with four undersized culverts are threatened by potentially large runoff and erosion events (due to large contiguous patches of high soil burn severity in the watershed), the VAR valuation process would first calculate the B/C ratios for the market VAR—road surface, culverts, and loss of road use for forest management and recreation. Assuming that the assessment of market VAR results in a B/C ratio of 0.6, the difference in the total treatment costs ($250,000) and the expected benefits of the treatments to the market VAR ($150,000) is assigned as the treatment costs to the non-market VAR ($250,000 - $150,000 = $100,000—the proportion of treatment costs assigned to the non-market VAR in this map zone). Assuming that the proposed treatments will reduce the probability of damaging sedimentation by 40 percent, the IMV of the non-market VAR (stream water quality and habitat suitability) is calculated as $100,000/0.4 = $250,000. The decision of whether the treatments are justified is based a determination of whether protection of the water quality of the stream reach in this Map Zone is worth at least $250,000 to the public.

Publishing Services Staff

Managing Editor · Lane Eskew

Page Composition & Printing · Nancy Chadwick

Editorial Assistant · Loa Collins

Contract Editor · Kristi Coughlon

Page Composition & Printing · Connie Lemos

Distribution · Richard Schneider

Online Publications & Graphics · Suzy Stephens

RMRS
ROCKY MOUNTAIN RESEARCH STATION

The Rocky Mountain Research Station develops scientific information and technology to improve management, protection, and use of the forests and rangelands. Research is designed to meet the needs of the National Forest managers, Federal and State agencies, public and private organizations, academic institutions, industry, and individuals. Studies accelerate solutions to problems involving ecosystems, range, forests, water, recreation, fire, resource inventory, land reclamation, community sustainability, forest engineering technology, multiple use economics, wildlife and fish habitat, and forest insects and diseases. Studies are conducted cooperatively, and applications may be found worldwide.

Research Locations

Flagstaff, Arizona	Reno, Nevada
Fort Collins, Colorado*	Albuquerque, New Mexico
Boise, Idaho	Rapid City, South Dakota
Moscow, Idaho	Logan, Utah
Bozeman, Montana	Ogden, Utah
Missoula, Montana	Provo, Utah

*Station Headquarters, Natural Resources Research Center, 2150 Centre Avenue, Building A, Fort Collins, CO 80526.